The
ANCIENT HEBI
NEVER DIE
Series

Book 4

Allah

The Most Misunderstood

Seyi Adebayo

**The
ANCIENT HEBREW NEVER DIED
Series**

Allah

The Most Misunderstood

**Psalm 24:1
(New International Version)**
*The earth is the LORD's, and everything in it, the world, and
all who live in it;*

COPYRIGHT

DEDICATION

To God Almighty, who makes all things good in his time

Benji, Baba & Becca

My forever crew, I know you are always there

Celia, Riona and friends, for showing the love of Christ
to us strangers

Brendan and Sharon, for bringing the light and the
music back into our lives, allowing this work that had
been put on hold to be resumed

I am so grateful for all the love and support you all gave.

PREFACE

Thank you for joining me and other readers on this journey of discovering Ancient Hebrew and its naturally-evolved forms as spoken by descendants of the Ancient Hebrews today. Over the course of this series, we will be exploring Biblical and Ancient Hebrew words, and their meanings in Modern Hebrew and Yoruba Hebrew, and the traditions of the speakers that match or mirror those of the Ancient Israelites as recorded in the Bible. I refer to this naturally-evolved form of Ancient Hebrew as Yoruba Hebrew so that readers will not confuse it with Modern Hebrew or Ancient Hebrew as translated without regard to Yoruba. Yoruba Hebrew is translated directly from Paleo-Hebrew which is earlier than the Aramaic script used in today's Modern Hebrew. Prince Oladipo Jejelola of Yoruba Torah Research Works discovered that vowelising Biblical Paleo-Hebrew with Yoruba vowels was yielding words that matched the KJV accounts on translation, and was also revealing additional information that was missing or mistranslated in the KJV. His work to complete the vowelisation and translation of the Bible directly from Paleo-Hebrew is ongoing. You can find out more about his work and how to support the translation work on Youtube and Facebook.

As I wrote in the first book of this series, the Ancient Hebrew language never died nor needed to be revived because Ancient Hebrew continued to be spoken by descendants of the Ancient Israelites through the ages, and like many languages across the world, Ancient Hebrew simply evolved. A hebrew remnant continued to speak their hebrew, through all the persecution, expulsions and the abduction and enslavement of their counterparts.

In this fourth book of the series, we will be looking at the Yoruba origins of the Arabic words for God. Many Yoruba Hebrews lived in today's Middle-East and Northern Africa before moving to join other Yoruba people in Sub-Saharan Africa, leaving as a result of religious persecution. Wherever the Hebrews lived they left an impression of their faith, language and culture, and the Islamic Quran and Hadiths are full of them - as we will see in this title and later ones in this series.

Please, note that the diacritical marks are made using General Yoruba, which may not accommodate all the tones from the various older dialects. The translation given of the word will assist the Yoruba reader in pronouncing correctly.

Seyi Adebayo
@ Home
31st March 2022

ACKNOWLEDGEMENT

My utmost gratitude is to *ELú Ọ̀YọHìíWàHá, ILàhà,* for the work he has started, and that I know he is faithful to complete.

My appreciation goes to all Researchers and Apologists on all sides, all contributors to related online forums, and everybody thirsty and working to find the truth in this mixed-up world. Your work and the knowledge shared and questions raised on your platforms contribute immensely to making connections and digging out the Yoruba hidden in Judaism, Christianity and Islam.

TABLE OF CONTENTS

Title …….....……….....…....…... 1
Copyright …………....….......… 2
Dedication ………....……....…… 3
Preface …………....……....…4 - 5
Acknowledgement …..............… 6
Table of Contents ……….........7
Chapter 1 …....................... 8 - 20
Chapter 2 …......................21 - 28
References …....................… 29
Pronunciation Guide….......30 - 33
About the Author…….............… 34

1 RETPAHC

Allah. This title evokes fear, hatred, submission, or love, depending on where you are looking at it from. Today, we won't concern ourselves with what he commands in the Qur'an and hadiths or what people do in his name but instead we will uncover the roots of this title, using - you guessed it - the Yoruba language.

Allah is known as the God of Islam, used both as an appellative and a proper name in the Qur'an. The name is used in Arabic to refer to God by both Muslim and Christian Arabs, and this usage points to the fact that the word Allah is not exclusively Islamic. It means that the title was in use in pre-Islamic times to refer to God or a god. A close word that is also used to denote God in Arabic is ***Ilaha***, and both words are found in the world-known Islamic expression '***La Ilaha ilaAllah'***, which is usually interpreted as follows:

'There is no god but God'
'There is no god but Allah'
'There is no deity but God'
'There is no deity but Allah'

The interpretation as given by Muslims has raised questions and will continue to do so for as long as no better interpretation is offered by the people of Allah. Some Arab muslims also tell us that the word Allah really means 'owner', and others tell us it means Lord'.

To find the meaning of Allah, let us first look at languages that share a bit in common with the language known as Arabic today for cognates:

Alaha - Aramaic
Aloho - Syriac
Eloah - Middle-Eastern Hebrew
Allah - Arabic

Allah is explained by some to be a combination of **AL** and **ILAH** but this explanation creates a problem for translating the expression **'La Ilaha ila Allah'** as it would then mean 'There is no god but The God' or 'There is no deity but The God', leaving us still wondering who ' The God' is, and what his name means.

Since Semitic names usually have meanings, these 'names' should plainly showcase their meanings, and be clear to many who know the particular language. It should not require a scholar or cleric to explain it. If Allah and any other Arabic names for a god/ God are 'Arabic' in origin, then many Arabs should be able to break it down and tell us their meanings. If you ever find the Arabic meanings, and can break it down and can use the broken components in sentences without losing those meanings, please kindly email me at hello@ahisay.com with the heading 'Book 4 - I found it'.

If Allah is of Arabic origins and means Owner, Lord or the God, surely, the Arabic language must be littered with Allah being used as a word that means these things even when speaking in English. For example, sentences such as this should be normal:

The Allahs / Al-Illahs are not to blame
The Allahs /Al-Illahs must be crazy
I am the Allah/ Al-ilah of this house
Submit a reference from your Land-Allah /Al-Ilah

Nah? Why not? Aren't the names supposed to be generic? They should cause no offence if they literally just mean a god, owner or a lord.

Allah is an 'arabicised' form of the Yoruba word *'Alaha'*. Isn't it Aramaic you say? The language known as Aramaic today, like Arabic, contains a good bit of Yoruba - as you will find out in this series. As a Yoruba word, name and title, *Alaha -* also pronounced *Ala'ah -* has a meaning and can be broken down in Yoruba, unlike in the 'arabic' language, as they borrowed this word from Yoruba and adapted it.

To show you the meaning of *Alaha*, I will break the word in two and deal with it under the components: *Ala* + Ha.

ALA

Ala = Olu = Oli = Oni = Eni = Ani = Ali = Eli = Elu = Ulu = Uli

All of the above mean 'owner' or 'Lord' in the various Yoruba dialects. They indicate Lordship over, ownership of, or possession of an object or attribute that is indicated in a suffixed word.

When you knock out the last vowels, you should be able to recognise in this group one or more letter words that have been claimed to mean God/Lord/King in various Ancient Languages: *AL = OL = OL = ON = EN = AN = AL = EL = EL = UL = UL*

I can demonstrate the above with hundreds of examples showing that the three and two letter versions feature in day-to-day Yoruba speech, indicating ownership, possession or lordship but I will limit to a handful.

AL / ALA as Indicator of LORDSHIP and ceremonial OWNERSHIP of domain (Titles of some Obas and Baales in Yorubaland)

1. **Ala**ketu of Ketu (lt. Owner-Ketu of Ketu)
2. **Ala**afin of Oyo (lt. Owner-Palace of Oyo)
3. **Ala**jase of Ajase (lt. Owner-Ajase)

4. **Al**ake of Egbaland (lt. Owner-Ake of Egba) *Ake is one of his domains
5. **Al**afao of Afao (lt. Owner-Afao of Afao)
6. **Al**ara of Aramoko (lt. Owner-Ara of Aramoko) *Aramoko is also known as Ara
7. **Al**are of Ilare (lt. Owner-Are of Ilare) *Are is short form of Ilare
8. **Al**ato of Ato (lt. Owner-Ato of Ato)
9. **Al**ayegun of Ayegun (lt. Owner-Ayegun of Ayegun)
10. **Al**aye of Aye (lt. Owner-Aye of Aye)

AL /ALA expressed in the form of OL, ỌL, ON, EL, and *EL* as Indicator of LORDSHIP and ceremonial OWNERSHIP of domain (Titles of some *Obas and *Baales in Yorubaland)

11. **ỌL**owo of Owo (lt. Owner-Owo of Owo)
12. **OLU** of Igbo-ora (lt. Lord of Igbo-Ora)
13. **EL**emure of Emure (lt. Owner-Emure of Emure)
14. **ON**isan of Isan (lt. Owner-Isan of Isan)
15. **ỌL**oye of Oye (lt. Owner-Oye of Oye)
16. **ỌL**ogotun of Ogotun (lt. Owner-Ogotun of Ogotun)
17. **ẸL**ekole of Ikole (lt. Owner-Ikole of Ikole)
18. **OL**ugbo of Ugbo-Nla (lt. Owner-Ugbo of Ugbo-Nla)
19. **EL**eruwa of Eruwa (lt. Owner-Eruwa of Eruwa)

20. **OL**ufon of Ifon (It. Owner-Ifon of Ifon)
21. **EL**eriti of Eriti (It. Owner-Eriti of Eriti)
22. **ON**ipele of Ipele (It. Owner-Ipele of Ipele)
23. **ON**iba of Iba (It. Owner-Iba of Iba)
24. **ON**Ipopo of Popo (Benin Republic) (It. Owner-Popo of Popo)
25. **ONI**sabe of Sabe (Benin Republic) (It. Owner-Sabe of Sabe)

*My apologies to all the Yoruba traditional rulers whose titles are not listed. *The domain of the ruler is usually listed after the Title as some titles are borne by more than one ruler.

*Ọba = General title used for a Yoruba King;
* Baálẹ̀ = General title used for the head/ ruler of a smaller domain

The 'chameleonic' nature of the letters fixed in Proto-Semitic and Hebrew as **EL** and how it seamlessly morphs into **IL, AL, UL, OL, ỌL, EN,** and **ON** in the Yoruba dialects - as shown in the Titles above - without losing its meaning of Lordship/ownership has eluded translators of Middle-Eastern Semitic languages.

Every one of the titles listed above identifies the bearer as the King/Lord / Owner of the domains they rule over. The prefix ALA will morph into EL, OL, ON, ỌL and ỌN etc as shown above for ease of pronunciation. The next letter may be omitted through contraction, or it can take on the first letter of the 'conjoining' domain name

13

through crasis for the same reason, or take on the first letter of the morphed suffix for ease of pronunciation. Examples are as follows:

The titles 'ALAketu, ONisan and ELekole - official titles for the Lord, King and Owner of Ketu, Isan and Ikole respectively - can be re-expressed as follows:

ALAKETU	ONISAN	ELEKOLE
ONIketu	^^	ONI'kole
ENIketu	ENisan	ENIkole
EN'ketu	EN'san	EN'kole
EN'LIketu	EN'Lisan	EN'Likole
OONIketu	OONI'san	OOL'ekole
OLIketu	OLI'san	OL'Ikole
ALIketu	ALIsan	OL'Ikole
ELIketu	EL'Isan	ELI'kole
Olu Ketu	OLU Isan	OLu Ikole

AL / ALA as Indicator of ownership, possession or attribute

26. **Al**ápẹ̀rẹ̀ (lt. Owner-basket)
27. **Al**ágbàdo (lt.Owner-Corn) = Cornowner, Cornseller
28. **Al**áìsàn (lt. Owner-unwell) = The Sick
29. **Al**áànú (lt. Owner-mercy) = The Merciful
30. **AL**àـàyè (lt. Owner-living) = The Living
    *Life =aye
31. **AL**áre (lt. Owner-vindication) = The vindicated
32. **AL**áìní (lt. Owner-not having) = The Poor
33. **AL**ákùkọ (lt. Owner-Cockerel) = Cock-Owner, Cock-Seller
34. **AL**ufa (lt. Owner-Ifa) = Priest
35. **AL**ákọ́wé (lt. Owner-writer'book) = Educated, Letter-Writer
36. **AL**ágbára (lt. Owner-might) = Mighty, Strong
37. **AL**álẹ̀ (lt. Owner-ground) = Founder, Ancestor, Spirit being, Landowner
38. **AL**áyọ̀ (lt. Owner-joy) = The Joyful
39. **AL**ábá (lt. Owner-settlement) = Settlement Owner, Settlement founder
40. **AL**áròyé (lt. Owner-explanation) = Talkative
41. **AL**ántàkùn (lt. Owner-weaving thread)= Spider
42. **ALÁL**ùpàyídà (lt. owner-owner-power of changing appearance) = Magician

Do you notice similarities in structure of the above with any 'Semitic' language?

AL / ALA as Indicator of ownership, possession or attribute, expressed in the forms of OL, ON, EL, EN, ẸL, ỌL and ẸL

43. *OLóyin* (lt. **Owner**-honey)
44. *ELékùrọ́* (**Owner**-kernel)
45. *ELélùbọ́.* (lt. **Owner**-yam flour)
46. *ẸLẹ́ran* (lt. **Owner**-meat)
47. *OLóbì* (lt. **Owner**-kolanut)
48. *ONÍbàtá* (lt. **Owner**-shoe)
49. *ELépo* (lt. **Owner**-Oil)
50. *ỌLọ̀pá* (lt. **Owner**-Staff/ Baton) = Policeman
51. *OLóyún* (lt. **Owner**-pregnancy) = Pregnant Person
52. *ON'sègùn* (lt. **Owner**-herbal works) = Herbalist
53. *EN'bàrà* (lt. **Owner**-buyer) = Customer
54. *ON'nòmọ̀* (lt. **Owner**-beef)
55. *ẸLẹ́gùsí* (lt. **Owner**-melon seed)
56. *ẸLẹ́yin* (lt. **Owner**-egg)
57. *ẸLẹ́yẹlé* (lt. **Owner**-pigeon)
58. *ANíkúlápó* (lt. **Owner**-death in pouch)
59. *ỌLọ́rọ̀* (lt. **owner**-wealth) = Wealthy one
60. *ẸLẹ̀dá* (lt. **owner**-creation) = God, the creator
61. *ỌLọ́run* (lt. **owner**-heaven) = God of heaven

*Where applicable, same word usually describes a owner and seller e.g. Egg-owner and Egg-Seller = *ẸLeyin*.

HA

In the dialects of the various peoples of the Yoruba 'hill country' in South Western Nigeria, there exists the word '*ihà*', that means 'existence'; it can also be used to mean character or 'being in a particular state'. Variations of this word in other Yoruboid dialects are *iwà* and *ùwà.* For the purposes of the word **Aláhà**, we will stick with 'existence'. It is this *ihà* that gets shortened to *hà* - for reasons shown under the next heading. Note that many Yoruba people will open and close vowels with an 'h', meaning words like *ihà, iwà* and *ùwà* will be pronounced as *hìhà, hìwà* and *hùwà or ihàh, iwàh* and *ùwàh,* but the voiced or half-voiced 'h' will be left out in writing Modern Yoruba because of spelling rules, even when they will be have to be used when writing older Yoruba dialects to allow correct reading.

ALAHA

How do ALA + IHA become ALAHA? It's similar to how AL+ ILLAH can become ALLAH. The process is called **IPAROJE** (lt. the killing of a sound) in Yoruba, known as 'contraction' in English Language. In ALAHA, the 'i' sound starting *'iha'* has been 'killed' but the meaning OWNER + EXISTENCE is still retained. The word **Aláhà** means **Owner of Existence, Lord of Existence.** For Yoruba people who close their vowels, **Alaha** will be pronounced **Alá'àh**. Imported into a 'foreign' tongue, the pronunciation of **Alá'àh / Aláhà** will most likely change.

When some Arabs say **Al(l)a(h)(a)** means Owner or Lord, it tells me that Yorubas had contact with the 'Arabs' long before the 14th Century 'first contact' claimed by some in the mainstream, under the name Yoruba or another. Page 131 of the book 'From Babylon to Timbuktu' writes about the presence of 'Yoruba Jews' in "the Ondo district of Nigeria who speak a mixture of Maghrebi Arabic and local Negro speech" who say their ancestors migrated from Morroco and had been driven from from place to place by Moslem persecution. There are other groups in Yorubaland and neighbouring areas who have traditions of migration from Yemen, Egypt, Iraq, North Africa etc having fled religious persecution.

ALAHA IN MODERN YORUBA

The equivalent of **Aláhà** in 'clear' Modern Yoruba is a word/ name you would have come across at least once before. It is **Olúwa.** A simple Facebook check will bring you lots of Yoruba people whose names are prefixed or suffixed with **Olúwa** or its shorter form **'Olú'**.

If you have been following me, you will remember that **Olú** is a dialectal variation of **Alá;** and **ìwà** is a dialectal variation of **ìhà.** The same contraction rules applied in

Aláhà result ***Olúwa*** from **Olú** + **Ìwà**. The meanings are the same: Lord/Owner of Existence.

ALAHA AS CAN BE RE-EXPRESSED IN OTHER WAYS/ DIALECTS IN YORUBA WITH THE MEANING RETAINED

1. OLuwa	2. Eeliha / Eeliah
3. Eloha / Eloah	4. EiLiha / EiLiah
5. Oluha / Oluah / Olugha	6. Eyi Li'ha
7. Ala'ah / Alaha	8. Hii Li'ha
9. Eluwa	10. Hii Lu'ha / Hii L'uwa
11. Eluiwa	12. Yee Lu'ha / Yee L'uwa
13. Elugha	14. Ei Lu'ha
15. Eluigha	16. Eelu'ha /Eeluah
17. Eloigha / Eloiha / Eloiah	18. Eelu'wa
19. Aloha / Aloah	20. Ailiah / Ailiah
21. Alugha	22. Aluha / Aluah
23. Oluiwa	24. Aluwa
25. Aliha / Aliah	26. Oliha / Oliah
29. Oyo Li'ha	30. 'Yi L'uha
31. Yee Li'ha	32. 'Yi Liha

*'ah' and 'ha' are swappable, and feature alongside 'wa' in the dialects of the 'hill country' areas of Western Nigeria. Other areas use 'wa'.

Just as Marwa (Arabic) and Moriah (ME Hebrew) refer to the same mount, Eluwa (Yoruba) and Eloah (Yoruba, ME Hebrew) refer to the same Lord of Existence, as do all other variations as listed above.

2 RETPAHC

ILAHA

You may still be unsure that **Allah** is an 'arabicised' form of the Yoruba **Aláhà** (also **Alá'àh)** but you must have noticed the similarity of **Aláhà** with the 'arabic' **ILaha.** The first noticeable difference between **Alaha** and **ILaha** is as clear as day, in that the first letters are not the same, being 'A' and 'I' respectively.

In Yoruba,

     a. *Alí/Ali* = Own**er** / **One Who** owns (has/does/can)
     b. *Hìí li* = **The One Who** owns
     c. *Hìí Lì ìhà* = The one who owns existence
     d. *ÍLìhà* is a 'contraction' of *'Hii Li'ha'* / *'Hii Li iha'*

     e. *ALá / AL'* = Own**er**
     f. *ILí / IL'* = **One Who** owns
     g. *AL'ihs* / *AL'aha* / *ALi'ha* / *ALa'ha* / *IL'iha* / *IL'aha* / *ILi'ha* / *ILa'ha* = **The One Who owns** existence

h. *AL*à = Bring**er**-about
i. *ÍL*à = The One Who **brought-about**
j. *Hìí* **L**à'*hà* = The One Who **brought-about**' existence
k. *ÍL*à*hà* is a 'contraction' of *'Hìí La ìhà'* / *'Hìí L*à*hà'*

l. *AL*à / = Bring**er**-about
m. *AL'* = Doer of / Able to do (the suffixed verb)
n. *AL'*à*hà* / *AL*à*'hà* = **The bringer-about** of existence

L*à *in* **h *to* **n** *is commonly used to portray 'emergence, appearance, breaking-out, breaking-forth'. *iLiah, iLa'ah are valid alternative Yoruba pronunciations of iLiha and iLaha respectively.*

The 'AL+ILLAH contraction to ALLAH' explanation given by some Muslims for Allah can be accommodated in Yoruba without contraction as seen directly below:

o. AL + ILAH(A) = ALILAH(A)
p. *ALILAH(A)* = owner brought-about existence / Person brought-about existence.
Dialectal and pronunciation variants for *AL*í*l*à*hà* (ah-lee-lah-ah): *ALila'ah* (ah-lee-laah), *ǪL*í*l*à*hà* (aw-lee-lah-ah), *ǪN*í*l*à*hà* (aw-nee-lah-ah), *EN*í*l*à*hà* (eh-nee-lah-ah), *EL*í*l*à*hà* (eh-lee-lah-ah), *EN'l*à*hà* (eh-n-lah-ah).

q. *ALAHA* and *ILAHA* are valid contractions of *ALILAHA* / ALILA'AH (AL +ILAHA aka AL + ILAH)

From **a** to **n** above, the Yoruba words *ÍLàhà, ÍLìhà, Aláhà* and their alternative pronunciations refer to the Ownership/Lordship of Existence but *ÍLàhà* emphasises 'Creation (bringing-about)' of that existence while *ALáhà* emphasises 'Ownership'. It is now important to bring to mind here that Allah is often referred to as the **Lord of the Worlds.** These worlds that Allah is the Lord of 'exist', meaning, they are part of 'existence'. This means *Allah (AliLaha, AliLah)* is expressing the same idea as *ÍLàhà* and *Aláhà,* as the 'Bringer-about', owner/ Lord, causer, 'doer' of creation.

Is today's Modern Yoruba *'Olúwa'* an equivalent of *Allah, ÍLàhà, ÍLìhà* and *ALáhà / ALá'àh*? Yes! In recent history, when Slavery and Indenture still existed in Yorubaland, the Master or owner of a slave was referred to as the 'Olúwa'. A king or a Chieftain would also be addressed by subjects as *'Olúwa* mi' - My **Lord**; a Yoruba woman would refer to her husband as her *Baálé* , but could potentially refer to her husband as her *'Oluwa'* because he paid her 'bride price' and ceremonially 'owns' her. In the Courts of Law, the Yorùbá term for 'My **Lord**' is *'Olúwa* mi'. Yorùbá Christians, for the **Lord** Jesus, use 'Jesu *Olúwa'*, or *Olúwa*. In Modern Yoruba, for the Arabic *'La ilaha* *ill**Allah**'*, Yoruba Muslims say *'Kò sí Oba kan àyàfi **Olúwa'*** which word for word translates as 'Not is/be King one except (The) Lord'. They sometimes use **Ọlọ́hun** instead of **Olúwa**. This is the *'**Alahan'*** you find in 'Aramaic', which is an alternative pronunciation in some Yoruba dialects, and may sound closer to **Ọlọ́hun** when pronounced or in between. **Ọlọ́hun** is **Ọlọ́run**, the Owner/Lord/God of heaven, and is written as the latter in Modern Yoruba taught in Nigerian schools.

*'La ilaha ill**Allah**'* is arabised from Yoruba. In one or more older Yoruba dialects, *'Lá, **ÍLàhà** í L'**Aláhà'*** word for word translates as 'No/Never, **The-bringer-about-(of)-existence** this-one is' **The-owner-(of)-existence'**. This translation shows that *ÍLàhà* means the same as the Mosaic YHWH *(oYo-Hii-iWa-Ha)* **'The bringer-out (of)-that which-exists-forth'.** I already covered the meaning of YHWH in an earlier Book. The expression *'Lá, **ÍLàhà** í L'**Aláhà'*** is essentially saying that 'No, this YHWH is The Lord of Existence'. This one YHWH is the Lord of the worlds, this one YHWH - not any other- is the Lord of all creation, this our YHWH that we already know is Lord over all! The expression appears to have been coined in the early days of Islam in response to an attempt to impose an image of/ or other persons / gods as God. Something in history triggered this phrase! Doesn't Islam reject the notion of anybody else being God alongside God or being an associate with God?

Hii + La + iHa = i + La + Ha
The one who + Brought-about + existence
The one who brought about existence

Y + H + W + H = oYo + Hii + iWa + Ha
The Bringer-out + That Which + Existence + Forth
The one who brought out existence

If you are fluent in Arabic, and do not accept what I have put before you, I challenge you to show from 'Arabic' the same as I have done so far in this book with Yoruba. Break down the words *ILaha, Allah, Al + ilah(a)* and *Alaha, Ala'ah* in Arabic, and give examples of Arabic usage of those components with the meanings retained. It is important that you break the words down in Arabic to show that they are 'Semitic' and native to the Arabic language. Before you do so, let me advise you that the Yoruba in 'Arabic' is not limited to *ILaha, Ala'ah / Allah* or *Al ilaah*. In the course of this series, I will show you how 'Quranic Arabic' and spoken Arabic contain plenty of 'Arabicised' Yoruba (Hebrew) language. Words and phrases like, Jihad, Hijab, Wallahi Tallah, Sumobillah, Baitullah, Quran, Kaaba, Abdul, As-Sajdah, Rasul, Akbar, Dawah etc are arabicised from one or more Yoruba words. Claims of Arabic loan words into Yoruba by Western scholars and Yoruba Muslim Scholars should be carefully examined as the traffic appears to be the other way round.

How did Islam end up 'adopting and adapting' a Yoruba word for the name of God? Why a Yoruba word that avoids directly saying 'YHWH' but re-expresses in a form that means the same just like the Yoruba language, thought and culture allow? Simply because Yoruba-speaking hebrews (including Yoruba-speaking 'Arabs') who were multilingual were there at the beginning of Islam before it was hijacked and all sorts of racist, anti-christ and sexual perversion elements were introduced into the Islamic documents and idealogy. These elements themselves are not practised by Yoruba Muslims today, and will never be discussed in public amongst the general Yoruba populace as being acceptable. They are one of the most peaceful and welcoming people in the world and you will not find Islamic terrorism in Yorubaland by Yoruba Muslims because such is regarded as abominable and considered 'mixing madness with religion'.

Why does *ÍLàhà* have the same meaning as YHWH? This is simply because YHWH was at the beginning of Islam, YHWH was the God of the original founders of Islam. This God is misunderstood for someone else today because Islam morphed into what we see today along the way. The commandments of Prophet Mohammed's *ILaha* and Jesus's YHWH are on two different ends of a scale, mostly, and the character and deeds of Prophet Mohammed as described in the Hadiths is the opposite of Jesus Christ's as described in the Christian scriptures, and following the commandments of one means going against the commandments of the other. Allah is misunderstood because of what politico-religious ideology claims he is.

Allah is misunderstood because those who preach the hatred, enslavement and annihilation of those who don't follow his 'last messenger' portray him in a way that is different to what is known from the 'previous' Books sent by him'. Allah has been re-fashioned from a God who chose a certain people and gave instructions as to worship and living, to one who commands the hatred, enslavement and annihilation of those same people. *Alaha*, the *Ílàhà* whose right arm brought salvation to the entire world because of his chosen people erring, is re-modelled into Allah, the *Ílàhà* who has sent another group of people to violently subjugate the chosen people and the entire world, and tax or strike at their necks if they don't accept this shocking version of him. Allah, the *Ílàhà* dressed in the garb of the Islamic Narrative, crowned with the 'arabic' translation of the Qur'an, seated on a throne of Hadiths, holding a sceptre of Fatwas, surrounded by a host of transparent wide-eyed Houris destined as gifts for Islamic martyrs for their everlasting carnal gratifications, is far from recognition as the **ELú** of Abraham, Isaac and Jacob, the YHWH of Moses, and the **ELoi** of Jesus. The Islamically-robed Allah is not a moon-god, his followers' love of the image of the crescent moon, and adornment of places of his worship with images of the moon, and their historical worship of an *ÍLàhá* - a *'riser-forth'*, the moon in this case - creates a misunderstanding of him as a Moon-god! The misunderstanding is caused by the false claims of Islamic Narrative regarding the Arabic language.

Hìí-Là-há is ~~The~~ One who + rises + forth, while *Hìí-Là-hà* is ~~The~~ one who + brings-about + existence. The difference is as a result of the diacritical marks determining whether '*ha*' is read as 'forth' or 'existence'. The reading of the 'ha' then determines whether the 'Là' is interpreted as 'rises' or 'brings about'.

Allah is not evil; the ungodly ideology padded with fabrications and riding on the back of this title of the *Alá* of Abraham is.

I hope that you have learnt something new, and that you will join me again on the next title in the series. Do feel free to follow me on Amazon so you get a notification of my new books. You can also contact me at hello@ahisay.com or support my work via
CASH APP Cash Tag: £AncientHebrew or
PATREON: https://www.patreon.com/ancienthebrew.

Till next time, I pray the *ìBu-iRe-KHún* of *ELú Ọ̀YọHìíWàHá, ILàhà,* upon you and all yours.

References

https://biblehub.com/niv/psalms/24-1.htm
Rudolph R. W, 1969, From Babylon to Timbuktu, Pg 131

Pronunciation Guide

Visit https://ahisay.com/pronunciation or see the YouTube Channel 'Ancient Hebrew Never Died' for the relevant videos.

Please, note that the diacritical marks are made using General Yoruba, which may not accommodate all the tones from the various older dialects. The guide helps the Yoruba reader to read correctly and identify the dialect in those cases.

ẹ as in Red

1. *Àiliàh = Ah-ee-lee-ah*
2. *Àilìhà = Ah-ee-lee-hah*
3. *ALá = (ah-lah) bringer-out*
4. *ALà = (ah-lah) owner*
5. *ALàhà = ah-lah-hah*
6. *ALáhà = ah-lah-hah (owner of existence)*
7. *Aláhan = ah-lah-hahn / ah-law-hahn / ah-lah-hoon / aw-lah-hahn*
8. *ALà'àh = ah-la-ah*
9. *ALá'àh = ah-la-ah (owner of existence)*
10. *Alí / Ali = ah-lee*
11. *Alìàh = Ah-lee-ah*

12. *Álìàh = Ah-lee-ee-ah / Ah-lee-ah*
13. *Álìhà = Ah-lee-ee-hah / Ah-lee-hah*
14. *Alìhà = Ah-lee-hah*
15. *ALílàhà = ah-lee-lah-ah*
16. *AlíLàhà = Ah-lee-(ee)-lah-hah*
17. *ALílà'àh = ah-lee-laah*
18. *AlíLà'àh = Ah-lee-(ee)-lah-ah*
19. *Álòàh = Ah-loh-ah / Ah-loo-ah*
20. *Álòhà = Ah-loh-hah / Ah-loo-hah*
21. *Alùàh = Ah-loo-ah*
22. *Álùàh = Ah-loo-oo-ah / Ah-loo-ah*
23. *Álùghà = Ah-loo-oo-ghah / Ah-loo-ghah*
24. *Alùhà = Ah-loo-hah*
25. *Álùhà = Ah-loo-oo-hah / Ah-loo-hah*
26. *Álùwà = Ah-loo-oo-wah / Ah-loo-wah*
27. *Alùwà = Ah-loo-wah*
28. *Aní = ah-nee*
29. *Èélìàh = ay-ay-lee-ah*
30. *Èélìhà = ay-ay-lee-hah*
31. *Èélùàh = ay-ay-loo-ah*
32. *Èélù'hà = ay-ay-loo-hah*
33. *Èélù'wà = ay-ay-loo-wah*
34. *Èí Lù'hà = eh-ee-loo-hah*
35. *ÈíLìàh = ay-ee-lee-ah*
36. *ÈíLìhà = ay-ee-lee-hah*
37. *Elí = ay-lee*
38. *ELílàhà = ay-lee-lah-hah*
39. *Elòàh = ay-loh-ah*

40. *Elòhà = ay-loh-hah*
41. *ELoi = ay-loh-ay-ee*
42. *Elóìàh = ay-lo-ee-ah*
43. *Elóìghà = ay-lo-ee-ghah*
44. *Elóìhà = ay-lo-ee-hah*
45. *ELú = (h)ay-loo*
46. *Elúghà = ay-loo-oo-ghah (half g + an h)*
47. *Elúìghà = eh-loo-ee-ghah (half g + an h)*
48. *Elúìwà = (h)ay-loo-ee-wah*
49. *Elúwà = (h)ay-looo-wah*
50. *Ení = ay-nee*
51. *EN'làhà = ęh-n-lah-hah*
52. *Èyí Lì'hà = ay-yee lee-ah*
53. *hìhà = (h)ee-hah*
54. *Hìí li = Hee-lee*
55. *Hìí Lì'hà = hee-ee lee-ah*
56. *Hìí Lù'hà = hee-ee loo-ah*
57. *Hìí L'ùwà = hee-ee loo-wah*
58. *Hìi-Là-hà = eee-lah-hah (bringer-out - existence)*
59. *Hìí-Là-há = eee-lah-hah (riser-forth)*
60. *hìwà = (h)ee-wah*
61. *hùwà = (h)oo-wah*
62. *ìBu-iRe-KHún = e-boo-e-ray-khoon / e-boo-e-ray-hoon / e-boo-e-ray-foon*
63. *ìhà = (h)ee-hah*
64. *ìhàh = (h)ee-hah*
65. *íLà = ee-lah*

66. *ILàhà = (ee)e-lah-hah*
67. *Ílàhá = (ee)e-lah-hah*
68. *ÍLà'àh = ee-lah-ah*
69. *ÍLi = ee-lee*
70. *ÍLiàh = ee-lee-ah*
71. *ÍL'ìhà / ÍLìhà = ee-lee-hah*
72. *ìwà = (h)ee-wah*
73. *ìwà = (h)ee-wah*
74. *ìwàh = (h)ee-wah*
75. *Olí = oh-lee*
76. *Olíàh = Oh-lee-ah*
77. *Olíhà = Oh-lee-ee-hah*
78. *Olú = oh-loo*
79. *Olúàh = oh-loo-ah*
80. *Olúghà = oh-loo-oo-ghah (half g + an h)*
81. *Olúhà = oh-loo-hah*
82. *Olúìwà = Oh-loo-ee-wah*
83. *OLúwa = oh-loo-wah*
84. *Oní = oh-nee*
85. *Ulí = oo-lee*
86. *Ulú = oo-loo*
87. *ùwà = (h)oo-wah*
88. *ùwà = (h)oo-wah*
89. *ùwàh = (h)oo-wah*
90. *Yee Li'ha = 'Yay-ay lee-hah*
91. *Yèé Lù'hà = Yay-ay-loo-hah*
92. *Yèé L'ùwà = Yay-ay-loo-wah*
93. *Yí Lìha = 'Yee lee-ha*

94. *Yí L'ùha = 'Yee loo-ha*
95. *ẸLílàhà = ẹh-lee-lah-hah*
96. *ẸNílàhà = ẹh-nee-lah-hah*
97. *ỌLílàhà = aw-lee-lah-hah*
98. *ỌLọhun = aw-law hoon*
99. *ỌLọ́run = aw-law-roon*
100.   *ỌNílàhà = aw-nee-lah-hah*
101.   *Ọ̀yọ Lìhà = Aw-yaw lee-hah*
102.   *Ọ̀YọHìíWàHá = oh-yaw-eee-ee-wah-hah*

ABOUT THE AUTHOR

Seyi Adebayo is a British-Nigerian of *Yorùbá* heritage, with an educational background in Accounting and Law. She loves research, singing, writing, domains, and family life.

She can be contacted at: hello@ahisay.com , and her work supported via:
CASH APP Cash Tag: £AncientHebrew
PATREON: https://www.patreon.com/ancienthebrew

Printed in Great Britain
by Amazon

79122341R00031